LIVING THROUGH OBSTACLES

LIVING THROUGH OBSTACLES

A BOOK THAT PEOPLE CAN RELATE TO

CHERRYL OLIVER

This book is in honor of my beautiful Loving Mother, Jeanette. I would like to thank you for being there for me throughout my life and for being a great mother to me. You are my hero and my inspiration. You have been a great mother to all of your children. I would not have made it without you! I love you to the moon and back!

CONTENTS

LIFE

Well, life is definitely a challenge. Life is filled with trials and tribulations. For me, that is an understatement. I have had far too many trials and tribulations.

I was "the baby" or shall I say, I am still the baby of the family. I had a very good childhood. Adulthood has been a challenge. I enjoyed being the "baby of the bunch." It was great, and I got what I wanted. My Mom was my backbone and I really realized this later in life. With my Mom, I had strength and I thought that I could do anything. Mom was my everything.

My sister, Kaci, and I took dancing lessons. I enjoyed dancing and being the center of attention. I enjoyed dancing with my sister and the older girls. During one dance recital, I was in the front and I danced with my sister and the older girls when I was little. I was leading the pack

and it was fun. We also took part
in parades. We, little ones, rode in the back of a truck while my sister and the older girls danced and walked in the parades. That was fun, too. When in school, I remembered thinking that I wanted to perform and do something in front of large audiences as a child. Maybe, it can still happen. I used to perform and dance in programs at my big sister, Stacey's college and perform in front of large audiences in other programs, and it was fun! I enjoyed it!

My brother, Keith, took me trick-or- treating on Halloween. He drove me around in his white Volkswagen. He took me around in our neighborhood and outside of it. Keith would stop me from time to time at people's houses that I didn't know, and I told him that I didn't know them, and he told me to go knock on the door anyway. Well, that was adventurous.

Our family dog was Blacky. Blacky was our favorite dog. He was a black German Shepherd. Blacky was a very smart dog. His favorite pastime was to chase cars and look after me and the family. He was our protector. Not only did Blacky protect us, but he looked after our neighbors, too. Blacky knew who lived in our neighborhood. Blacky took care of me, and he was my bodyguard. Blacky got after my brother when he tried to whip me. I loved that dog! Daddy got rid of our dog because Blacky got after him; I think Daddy was going to whip me, and Blacky protected me then. That was a solemn day in our household. We were so sad. Our dog was my bodyguard. My brother was doing something to me and Blacky protected me and got after him. I remembered Blacky to this very day. He was a great dog. Blacky was the best dog that we ever had.

These were the good ole days. My best days were when I was small and attending Russell Kindergarten and grade school. I did not have a care in the world. I got whatever I wanted. My childhood days were my better days. I was the "baby of the bunch," and my brother and sisters were teenagers; they were courting and out with their friends. They would spend some time with me, too. I use to ask my sisters to read to me because I liked it when others read to me, but my big sisters didn't have time for that; they were too busy courting, running around the house, on the telephone, and doing everything else. I liked it when my brother brought his girlfriend to the house. I would ask her to read to me, and she would. I enjoyed those special moments. Every time my brother and his girlfriend came to our house and walked through the front door, I would have my book in my hand. I guess his girlfriend knew that it was "reading time." Before you knew it, my big sisters went off to college, and my big brother got married and was doing his own thing. Then, it was Dad, Mom and me. It wasn't bad, though. I would still see my brother and my sisters. My sisters would come home from time to time from college. I missed my sisters a little bit.

My Mom and I hung out a lot. It was just us two. I enjoyed hanging out with my Mom. Even now, I like hanging out with my Mom like the ole days. My Mom took me to the "Drive-In" to see the movie, "Grease" with John Travolta and Olivia Newton- John one evening. We got hotdogs, popcorn, and soda for our refreshments. The movie was very good. The movie seemed to have lasted a long time, or it seemed that way. My Mom fell asleep during the movie. When the movie was over, I remembered saying, "Mama, wake up, people are leaving" and cars were pulling off. It was a good thing that I didn't fall asleep. We would have been in trouble.

My sisters were off to Alabama State University. My Mom,

Dad, and I took them to college a couple of times. I remembered running up and down the hallway of Bessie Benson Dormitory.

Stacey, my big sister, took me to class with her one day, and it was so boring. The class lasted a very long time. Needless to say, I did not go with her to her next class. Instead, I stayed with one of her friends in the dormitory while Stacey went to her next class. Well, while I was in the room with her friend, the roommate threw a radio and hit the wall because she was mad at something. I got the heck out of that room. I went down stairs to my sister's room by that time Kaci, my other sister, was in the room. When Stacey got out of class, I told her about it. I told her that those girls were crazy and that I was never going back to their room. I was in the fifth grade. Stacey and I went to the cafeteria. I ate her lunch. I was experiencing "college life" early.

Stacey got married soon after college. She had a big wedding. The church was packed. Everybody knows my sister, Stacey. My Dad, Mom, Kaci, Keith, and I were in the wedding. I was a junior bridesmaid. The wedding reception was down to Annie Paul's Lodge. We had a good time. I danced with Kaci's boyfriend, a lot. I stood on top of his feet while we danced. Michael was Kaci's college boyfriend at that time. Everybody had a good time at the wedding reception. Our cousin, J.R.., Aunt Gloria's son, was the DJ at the wedding reception.

My Aunt Gloria would pick me up to go to the college

basketball games. Her son was a member of the basketball team. Aunt Gloria is my Mom's sister. I enjoyed going to the basketball games. It was fun. I also enjoyed getting out of the house and having some excitement. On weekends, my Mom and I would go shopping and frequently go visit Aunt Gloria. I would always say, "Mom, let's go over Aunt Gloria's house."

I had a good childhood; it was great being the "little one." My Mom gave me several birthday parties. My Mom and sisters were the hosts at my parties. I had a party when I was in the fifth grade. We played "Pin the Tail on The Donkey," "Musical Chairs," and other games. The best part was when everybody sang, "Happy Birthday" to me and I blew out the candles on the cake and I opened up my presents.

My Christmases would be very special as well. My Christmases and other days were filled with love and a lot of presents. I always had a very good Christmas. My Christmases now are special when I spend them with my family, although I don't get gifts like I did when I was little and in my Mom's house. My Mom Christmas decorations would be Lit. She would have the block lit up, and the house would be so pretty inside and outside! People in our neighborhood and throughout the city would be excited every year to come by our house to see my Mom's Christmas decorations. Christmas was an exciting time for all of us. Christmas was my Mom's favorite Holiday. Mom would bake her famous cakes and the house would be filled with fantastic aromas of Christmas and her cakes, and Dad would go and get fruit, oranges and apples, and peppermint candy. Dad loves his peppermint candy and Mom loves her specialty cakes, Lane Cake and fresh Coconut Cake which she makes at Christmas time. Mom would get busy decorating our house with her Christmas trees, reindeers, Mr. &

Mrs. Santa Claus, beautiful Christmas lights, and more! Everybody would be in a great mood and enjoyed Christmas.

Each year, people would come from afar just to see my Mom's Christmas decorations. They would be so pretty. My Mom would have the best Christmas Decorations in the city.

I was a Girl Scout. My Mom would take me to Girl Scout meetings. I would have to pay my Girl Scout dues. I learned quickly that I was not an outside camping person. There were no restrooms outside. I could not wait until the next morning when my Mom came to pick me up. Boy, I was happy to see her! You could only imagine. You would have thought that I had left her for a while. I was only gone for one evening. That was a long night for me.

On several occasions, my Mom, Dad, and I would go to Atlanta to visit my Aunt Bobbi, my Mom's sister. Sometimes, my Mom, Uncle Bill, my Mom's brother, Aunt Gloria, my Mom's sister, and I would go to Atlanta. We would have a good time on our trip.

In Junior high school, I was a basketball cheerleader. I liked to watch basketball and I liked to play basketball, too. I like to watch professional basketball games on TV. I have gone to watch the Atlanta Hawks in person. I still like to play basketball today or "shoot around." It is good exercise and it is fun. I also was the Treasurer of the Student Council. I ran against three other opponents. I campaigned for weeks. I, along with my friends, made campaign signs and buttons. I made a fantastic speech. I ended my speech with this fantastic phrase, "Bees are in charge of honey, so let me be in charge of the money." That was cool! Everybody in the school loved it! Yes, I WON! I was now the Student Government Treasurer. I beat out the three opponents. We had an election. We went into voting booths at the school and voted just like you do in a government election.

I was the Head of the finance department. We sold candy and other goods to raise money for special events and the school. I also went to the junior high school proms in the eighth and ninth grade. I was invited by someone on the Student Council in the eighth grade, and in the ninth grade, I was eligible to go and invite someone.

My Dad drove the school bus for many years. I had my very own VIP service. The advantage of this was that I could get on the bus when Dad got on, and I didn't have to wait on the side of the road and stand in the cold.

My Mom got home from work and would have cooked dinner by the time that Dad and I got home, off the school bus, in the afternoon. It was great to have a mom that had dinner prepared because I was good and hungry by the time that I got home from school. My Mom would sometimes cook my favorite meal: pinto beans, fried chicken, coleslaw, and cornbread. I love those days! I cannot forget the onions that I added on top of my pinto beans. Ummmmmm, the food would be delicious! I have a great Mom! My favorite is pinto beans and my Dad's favorite is butter beans.

On Fridays, I could not wait to get home from school. I would get home, go to my room, and throw my books on the floor. My Mom would be waiting for me to get home. We would go shopping. I enjoyed our Mom and Daughter times together.

As a high school student, one of the biggest highlights was getting my driver's license. I was sixteen. My Mom took me to get my Driver's License. This was very exciting. My Dad took me to get my Learner's Permit prior to me getting my Driver's License. I played basketball for one year. I would have been good if I had someone to work with me. All the other years, I attended the basketball games. It was really fun when our high school played our rivals, Goodwater and Dadeville, especially Goodwater High School. It was a packed house on those nights. Everybody knew to go to the game early in order to get a seat. I attended my Junior and Senior proms. Back then, they were boring because they never got a DJ that played good music. The biggest excitement at the school was going to these basketball games and Homecoming.

We played Dadeville every year for Homecoming. I remember my Mom ordered me some boots that I had wanted and I got a new outfit for Homecoming and I was also wearing my Homecoming Corsage that I received from a guy that liked me. That was real cool. I looked real pretty. I was also busy being in beauty pageants. I won one year. One of the biggest Senior highlights for me was getting an invitation in the mail from Alabama A&M University to attend "Senior Day." I also won a gift that was sent to me in the mail. On Alabama A&M "Senior Day," we had an oriental breakfast, Orientation which we heard from the University President and Miss Alabama A&M University and later attended the football game between Alabama A&M University and Tuskegee University. That was fun. Alabama A&M University's Band played "The Show" by Doug E Fresh and that was/is one of my favorite songs. I will never forget it! "The Show" is still one of my favorite old school songs. It sounds real good! The band was bad as in good! I was ready to graduate from high school and start Alabama A&M University!

COLLEGIATE LIFE

I decided to attend Alabama A&M University. I am an Alabama A&M Bulldog for life. My Mom and Dad took me to college. That was a good day, but a sad one as well.

I remember sitting in the back seat of the car in our driveway when my Mom and Dad were about to drive me off to college for the first time. We left early, at about 5 a.m., in August. My sister, Kaci and Aunt Bobbi had come from Atlanta to see me off to college. I began to cry a little and sniffle because the car was actually pulling out of our driveway, and I was going away from home. My Mom asked, "What is wrong with you?" I replied, "I got a cold." I'm sure Mom knew that wasn't true. I'm sure she knew what was going on. As they say, Mama knows what is going on with her child. As we got on the campus of Alabama A&M University, we were met by my cousin, Jazzy and Aunt Vivian who is my Mom's sister. My cousin, Jazzy and I were roommates at Thigpen dormitory. This was the freshmen dormitory and the better dormitory of the two freshmen dormitories.

When my Mom and Dad pulled off, I started to cry again, but harder. I realized that I was sort of like on my own. This was a feeling like I can't explain. As my Mom and Dad were driving away in the car, my tears started coming down my face and I could not stop them.

As I looked around, I was standing there alone. I saw students walking around. I hurried to wipe away my tears, but I still had a wet face and red- shot eyes from crying. I began to walk to the dormitory. As I entered my room, there was my cousin, Jazzy. She was unpacking and doing last-minute things to arrange her side of the room. My cousin seemed to be doing fine. She hardly lets anything bother her. I don't guess it bothered her when her parents left. I guess that I am more of the emotional one of the two.

Well, life on "The Hill" had started for us. We proceeded to go to the cafeteria for lunch. Lunch was the best out of the three meals. We knew that we were going to have potatoes in some form for lunch. They always served potatoes for lunch. Often times, we would have chicken sandwiches and French fries. The cafeteria was usually packed for lunch. Usually after lunch, I would always have a class around 2:00 or 3:00, but my cousin would be relaxing and enjoying the rest of her day. It just seemed like she scheduled all her classes for the morning, but somehow, my schedule did not work out that way. Later on, she ended up with an afternoon class.

My cousin and I had completed a full week as freshmen at Alabama A&M University. That Friday, nobody was on "The Hill." I remembered talking to my Mama on the telephone. I said, "Mama, nobody is on this campus but Jazzy and me. Please come get us." My Mom told me that she was going to call me back. I can only imagine what was going through my Mom's mind because she and my Dad had just dropped me off on the previous weekend to start college. It was truly a ghost town. Every student had gone home after his or her first week. I guess all of the students were homesick. It was awful because it seemed as if Jazzy and I were the only students left on the campus and my Mom and Dad had just brought to the University a week before.

Well, I didn't hear from my Mom fast enough. So, I called her back. I pleaded with my Mom again to come and get us. Mom said that she was going to get J.R. to come get us. J.R. is my Aunt Gloria's son. J.R. had gone to Alabama A&M University, too. We were so happy to see J.R. and to go home. My Mom cooked us a home cooked dinner. It was delicious! As students, we longed for my Mom's home cook meals. Any student knows what I am talking about. Even if you are not a student, you always love your Mom's cooking. There is nothing like your Mom's home cook meals.

Jazzy and I enjoyed our Freshman and Sophomore years. We went to our classes and, of course, went to parties. We enjoyed the "Dust to Dawn" party which Alabama A&M University is known for on a Friday, a day before Homecoming. The "Dust to Dawn" party was in the old gym on the boys' end of the campus. The only thing that we hated was walking to the old gym, which seemed a long way when we were walking at night. But to be honest, I hated to walk to the old gym during the day because it was a long way from the girls' end of the campus to the boys' end. One thing about Alabama A&M University, you will get your exercise walking from class to class and building to building.

Life on "The Hill" was interesting for me. While a student at Alabama A&M University during my sophomore year, I pledged Alpha Kappa Alpha Sorority, Inc.

I wear a lot of pink and sometimes, I wear my "pink and green." I also wear my AKA paraphernalia. I represent! I look pretty in my "pink and green." Well, I look pretty in all colors. I was "Miss Alpha Kappa Alpha Sorority, Inc." My court and I was in the Homecoming Parade that year. I rode in one car and my court rode in another car behind me. It was cool! I had a fantastic time representing my sorority at Homecoming, the Inauguration Ball, and other events. My Mom, Dad and my brother came to Huntsville to see me in the Homecoming parade. My sister, Stacey, her husband, John, and their two sons, Mike, and Jay came to Huntsville to see me in the Homecoming Parade. I spent the evening with them.

I recently attended Homecoming. Alabama A&M University played against Tuskegee, again. I enjoyed the getaway and the opportunity to stroll, step and chant with my sorority sisters.

I was also an officer, Parliamentarian of Alpha Kappa Alpha Sorority, Inc. while a student at Alabama A&M University. We, AKA's were busy on campus. We had our AKA parties and much more. Of course, I represented. I had fun at the AKA parties. I enjoyed painting our AKA stone along with some other sorors. I enjoyed the other functions as well.

You can also catch me wearing my Alabama A&M University T-shirts and my Alabama A & M University Alumni T-shirts. How can I forget "The Magic City Classic?" My cousin and I would ride the student bus to "The Magic City Classic" while we were students at Alabama A&M. "The Magic City Classic" is the famous football game between my sisters' Alma Mater, Alabama State University and my Alma Mater, Alabama A & M University. This is like Alabama and Auburn. The rivalry takes place at Legion Field in Birmingham, Alabama, on the last Saturday in October. The Magic City Classic is the largest HBCU Football Game in the country. The Magic City Classic has been going on for almost 70 years and it is still going on strong. This is one of the "most exciting and famous" football classics of the Historically Black Colleges. My sisters and I attend the Magic City Classic a lot.

My nephew, Landon, attends the football games as well. He normally wears his "Black and Gold" representing his fraternity, Alpha Phi Alpha, Fraternity. I am an AKA, and my nephew is an Alpha. We are the First Fam. A lot of times, you can find me stunning in my AKA shirts and my pink and green.   My nephew is also a graduate of Alabama State University. His favorite sport is basketball, but he enjoys going to the football games, too. Like many others, We enjoy the half-time show between the bands, the Marching Hornets and the Marching Bulldogs. Sometimes, Alabama A&M wins, and sometimes, Alabama State wins. Last year, I can't remember which band was the best. I want to say, Alabama A&M's band because that is my school, but in all honesty, I can't remember. I actually enjoy hanging out with my sisters for "The Magic City Classic" weekends. A lot of people go to the football games to see the bands during the half-time show.

My Mom and Dad would attend "The Magic City Classic" too. My Mom's house is Half-In-Half. She has two daughters who graduated from Alabama State University and one daughter who graduated from Alabama A&M University. When my Mom attended the football game, she would be like Venus and Serena's mom. Mom would sit on Alabama A&M University side one year and sit on Alabama State University side the next year or sit on the fifty-yard line. She would wear a Half-in - Half T-shirt with Alabama A&M University on one side and Alabama State University on the other side or wear an Alabama A&M University baseball cap and an Alabama State University T-shirt. Maybe this is why she chooses to watch the football clips on the news.

MY EXPECTATIONS

I had very high expectations for my Life. I only wanted the best of things. Well, that is still true to this very day. I want the very best. When I graduated from A&M University Alabama with a B.S. Degree in Marketing, I knew that I was on my way to get a very good high-paying job that I deserved, but that did not happen as I planned. Well, I guess that I can say that things did not go as planned or as expected for a lot of things in my Life. I am now looking to do bigger things on a higher level. The sky is the limit!

I can speak to audiences and various groups. I can actually see myself being a TV Correspondent or TV Host. Going through life, I really start to see what I enjoy doing and what I would like to do.

Life is three things:

1. Life is unpredictable.
2. Life is difficult.
3. Life is too short to be unhappy.

And for me, Life is a learning experience, for I have learned a lot through life experiences.

I often think of the ole cliché that older people use; they say, "If you haven't gone through something, keep on living." Well, it is not just for the old people. Young people are saying this now. You don't have to be old to go through something, nowadays. Whether it is the economy, your job, spouse, other people, or something else, there are a lot of problems that are facing the young and old. And problems are abundant.

For some of us, Life is more difficult than for others. Although I have had high expectations, my Life has taken many different turns and detours. There have been different turns of events. I do believe that fate has taken over half of the events in my life. Sometimes, although I try hard to make something happen one way or go a certain way; it doesn't happen that way. If there are any bad apples in the bunch and there are, I always seem to have to work with those bad apples on the jobs.

As a kid, I envisioned doing something and performing on a stage in front of large audiences. Now, I wouldn't mind doing a little acting. I am still interested in being a TV Host. I just need the opportunity!

God is over-timing, too. I just have to say that there are a lot of things that I am not going to understand in Life because I truly don't. But I have to say that things have to look up, and there will be brighter days and a future ahead for me.

I will always strive to do my best in everything that I do. I am going to go after the things that I want in life. I've always said that I want to be in a position where I can buy whatever I want to and buy it whenever I want to.

Betty Wright has a song, "No Pain, No Gain." She says it

best. Betty Wright says, "In order to get something, you got to give something. In order to be something, you gotta go through something, No Pain, No Pain, No Gain." I like this song. This is my motto. I am now looking for my Gain.

MY MOM, MY HERO, MY SPECIAL LADY

My Mom is my Hero and my Special Lady. I am so blessed to have a Mother like mine. My Mother loved me and supported me throughout my life. Had it not have been for her, I would not have made it. I made some bad decisions, and some things happened out of my control. It is pretty safe to say that my Mom saved my life, too. Had I been homeless, I don't think that I would be here today and writing this book. I Thank God for my loving and supportive Mother.

I think the world of my Mother. She is my Light, my Hero, and my Inspiration. I enjoyed us doing the "The Wobble Wobble." Every time that I hear that song, I think about us dancing and doing "The Wobble Wobble." Every time that I make Spaghetti, I think of my Mom because Spaghetti is one of her favorite dishes. Sometimes, I would make Spaghetti and my

Mom would put her special touch to it! I wish that I could make her Spaghetti again.

My Mom is a very classy, strong, talented, and intelligent true Diva!!! My Mom can do anything.

If it weren't for my Mom, I would have fallen on my face a long time ago. I am grateful to have her as my Mom. I am not proud that I had to rely so much on her as an adult, but I am very grateful and blessed to have her love and support.

"THE LOVE OF MY MOTHER"

You can't define a Mother's love;
It's faith, hope and power,
It's wisdom and unselfishness,
Protection by the hour,
You can't define a Mother's love:
It's prayer true and sincere.
It's tenderness down through the
Years, it's joy unthinkable.
Joy and smiles instead of tears,
You can't define a Mother's love
It's faith that never grows dim.
Mother's love is changeless,
And never does she tire.
For each day she's fulfilling
All our needs require.
You can't define a Mother's love.
Mother only Mother
Was sent by heaven above
To fill hearts with gladness
With tenderness and with Love.
Thank you, Mother For all your
Prayers, your sleepless nights and
Your many words
Of encouragement; but most of all,
Thank you for my training and
For leading me to Jesus. There will
Never be another mother to fill your shoes.

I pray that I can only be half the Mother you were

And still are to us.

AUTHOR UNKNOWN

FRIENDSHIPS

I must say that I did not think that my Life would have had so many obstacles and setbacks. Adulthood has been a challenge. Yes, I know that Life is not easy, but I did not know that it would be this hard for me, either. I think about the bad situations and the bad people that I encountered in the past. Well, things have to get better. I never thought that my Life would have taken all these twists and turns, and detours. I am a smart, intelligent, and educated young lady with a college degree and who has what it takes to get the job done. Well, Life proved to be different for me. Life does not come with a crystal ball or a real 8 ball that tells you what decisions to make and what decisions not to make. You can have faith and believe that things will go a certain way for the better and things don't happen that way. All of these outcomes can affect your life. Some decisions will affect the outcome of your life.

One day, I was riding in my car and I saw a man who was standing on the street corner and homeless. I thought that could have been me. If it weren't for my Mom, it would have been me. All because I made a bad decision, I could have been on the street. That really hurt to see that man. Well, it would have hurt worse, if it was actually me. Wow! You never know what Life will bring you and what pathway Life will take you down. Due to bad decisions and things out of my control, it caused me to be in some bad situations. I guess some people can understand this. Life is not equipped with a crystal ball or a navigator. If it did, Life would have been different and mistake free.

When I hear the song, "Never Would Have Made It," by Marvin Sapp, I immediately think about my Mom. This song is so fitting because I never would have made it without my Mom. I love my Mom very much; she is very special to me. I thank God for my Mom.

In the midst of my storm, I thank God for these blessings. I have to know that the storms will eventually pass. But I am ready for them to go away and to receive prosperity and happiness.

When I hear the song "Still Here" by The Williams Brothers, it messes me up. I reflect on my Life and it says it all. But I am "Still Here" by the grace of my Mom and God.

My song now is "Get Up" by Mary Mary. This is what I have to do to reach my goals and dreams. It is not about what somebody else says; it's what I say. I have got to "Get Up."

In life, some people will act like they are your friends, but they aren't. They will accept gifts from you and are okay as long as you are doing for them. When it is time for them to do something and give back to you, they won't give you anything or show up to support you.

I had some friends in college and we remained friends after college. They are also my sorority sisters. I had gone home with these friends and met family members. We were friends for years. Two of these friends asked me to be in their weddings, and I agreed to be in it. I made sacrifices to be in their weddings and had prior engagements. I was actually in school and I did double work and asked my instructor to allow me to do my presentation earlier so I could be in the wedding. I should have not been in it because I wasn't appreciated and I never got a "Thank you" or a "Thank you" card from neither one of these friends or so-called friends. I didn't have to agree to be in their weddings or spend my money to be in their weddings, but I did. I was being a friend. I spent money for gas to travel five hours to get to be in their weddings and money for dresses, shoes, and I bought each of them a wedding gift which I didn't have to do. Again, they didn't say "Thank you" or give me a "Thank you" card for me participating in their weddings or the wedding gifts that I bought for them. Again, I got no appreciation. I didn't receive a phone call from them after the wedding.

When I got married, these friends didn't attend my wedding reception. My Mom gave me a beautiful reception fit for a queen. I truly felt like a Queen. Thank you, Mom. I sent them an invitation in the mail, but these friends didn't attend my wedding reception and neither one of these friends bought me a wedding gift, either. I felt good and had a nice time at my wedding reception.

I was a friend to these individuals, and they weren't friends to me! I was a friend , spent money on them, and supported them, but they weren't friends to me , they didn't spend any money on me, and didn't support me.

I supported them, but they didn't support me. If I supported them, they should have supported me! People will use you and get what they can get from you and don't give anything to you. You can be a friend to some people and they won't do right and be a friend to you. I'm not wasting any more time with fake friends. I need honest, caring, supportive and real friends around me.

One of the definitions of a friend is a person who has a strong liking for and trust in another. A true friend may be someone who accepts you unconditionally, helps you grow, supports you in tough times, and increases your ability to love yourself. You may also do these things for them, showing them they mean as much to you as you do to them and becoming a better friend.

20 QUALITIES OF A TRUE FRIEND:

1. Supportive - If you are graduating, getting married, having a wedding reception, you would have true friends who show up to support you, give you a gift, be in your wedding and take part in your wedding receptions and do whatever to support you as a true friend.
2. Loyalty – Loyalty is about standing up for each other, being there in times of need, and never betraying trust. It's the glue that binds friends together, through thick and thin.
3. Honesty – Honesty lets you see each other without distortions. A sincere friend doesn't sugarcoat the truth. It's this transparency that builds a genuine relationship.
4. Empathy – Empathy is the ability to understand and share a friend's feelings. It's putting yourself in their shoes and offering support.
5. Respect – Respect is a nod to each other's opinions. This is treating your friend as you'd like to be treated.
6. Trustworthiness – Trust is the unspoken pact that your friend won't spill your deepest secrets or flake on a planned movie night. Without trust, it's impossible to build a lasting connection.
7. Nonjudgmental – A nonjudgmental friend provides a safe space to be yourself without fear of criticism or ridicule.
8. Dependability – Quietly ensuring everything runs

smoothly. A dependable friend is your go-to person, always in the right place at the right time.

9. Generosity – Generosity is giving without expecting anything in return. It's the shared dessert, the unexpected compliment, or the selfless act that says I care.

10. Good listener – Being a good listener is the art of giving your undivided attention. It's about understanding and responding in a way that makes the other person feel heard. Good listeners tune in, turning casual chats into meaningful conversations.

11. Humor – Having laughter in a friendship is like having a personal stand-up comedian on speed dial.

12. Patience – Patience is the willingness to pause, reflect, and give time for clarity.

13. Encouragement – A true friend's encouragement is like having a roaring crowd at your own personal marathon. It's that "You've got this!" You got a bit of extra motivation.

14. Common interests – True friendship springs from shared hobbies and values.

15. Flexibility – Flexibility in friendship is all about give and take. It's about respecting each other's pace and needs.

16. 16. Positive attitude – It energizes conversations and turns mundane moments into enjoyable experiences. Even when the chips are down, an upbeat friend lifts you up.

17. Keeps secrets – Keeping secrets is the unspoken oath between friends, guarding each other's private confessions like a treasure chest.

18. Low-maintenance – Friends who are always there, no matter what, even if it has been a while since you last spoke to them.
19. Sincerity – Genuine and heartfelt, it reflects the authentic connection between friends.
20. Deep conversations – Deep conversations are the hidden depths of a friendship, where you open up about your dreams and fears.

For me, a friend has your back. A friend is one who you can depend on, one who cares about you and your well-being, one who helps you when you are in need, one who you can call and talk to no matter what time you call them, day or night, and they don't mind talking to you, listening to you or providing advice and support. A friend is one who calls you and checks on you to see how you are doing and one who you can confide in. A friend is one who supports you during your good times and your bad times. A friend is one who will help put a smile on your face and helps put you in a good mood.

After I had stopped hanging out with certain people, I realized that those people weren't really my friends. Friends should support me no matter what, and I can depend on them no matter what.

I want people around me who are genuinely good people, who I can depend on, who support me, and who know how to be a friend.

OBSTACLES

Life is a lot of things: Life is fun. Life is a blessing. Life is interesting. Life is a challenge. Life is unpredictable. Life is difficult. Life is short, so we all should live life to the fullest extent and go after our dreams. Sometimes, we have problems and focus more on our problems instead of focusing on our blessings. I am very grateful for my health, strength, and family. I am also grateful for each day that God allows me to wake up and gives me another chance to get it right, to go after what I want, or to make things better in my Life.

Sometimes, it gets really hard not to focus on our problems, especially when they deal with the essentials of life.

I had a very good childhood. Adulthood has been a challenge. Life is definitely unpredictable. Even at this point, I thought that I would be in a different situation. Like most young women and some men, I had done an outline in my head years ago of certain events and things that I wanted to accomplish by a certain age or time in my Life. Well, things did not go like that. There are a lot of things that I don't understand. Even though I was confident that certain things and events were going to take place in a given time, they didn't.

Sometimes, you can try as hard as you can and some things are just not going to happen. I believe that you can go after what you want in Life, but sometimes, it is timing or simply it just isn't going to happen. I believe that I wasted a lot of time just waiting on those certain opportunities when, in fact, I should have been more flexible and started working on other opportunities in the meantime. As you go through Life, you learn more from your past decisions and experiences. I do believe in trying. However, I am going to go after my dreams. If I Can Conceive It, If I Can Believe It, I Can Achieve It!

There are jealous, evil, and envious people in the world. These types of people exist everywhere. They exist on the jobs, churches, and other places.

One instance, I had a woman who wasn't even my supervisor and she was trying to act like she was over me; she was a wannabe. There are a lot of people like that; people who aren't over anyone not even themselves. My immediate supervisor instructed me to share my password and give it to another employee. First of all, NO ONE IS SUPPOSED TO KNOW YOUR PASSWORD AND YOU ARE NOT SUPPOSED TO SHARE YOUR PASSWORD. Everyone knows this. That is the point of having a password so no one would see or be able to change your information on the computer. I knew that this was going to be a disaster; this was going to be a setup for this employee to go in and put errors on my work on the computer to make it look as though I did it.

I knew that this was trouble, instantaneously. I told the supervisor that I was not comfortable sharing my password with another employee because this allows someone else to go behind me to enter erroneous information on my work and it reflects me. The piece of supervisor stated that it goes on me still because it was my computer.

That was stupid enough. Look at these people who are in charge. This one was an idiot. I have had a lot of idiots over me. Well, the supervisor gave my password to the other employee anyway.

Well, you guessed it! Sabotage! As I figured it would happen. People were sharing computer passwords. You don't do that. People in their right minds know that you don't do that. I informed the principal of the school and he did nothing about the employee changing my information on my computer. I told him that I was being sabotaged. I even showed him proof; I printed off the information that I had entered in the computer and the copies of the receipts that I had written. Although I had proof that she had changed information on my computer, the principal did not fire her or discipline her. This employee did not stop there; she stole $40.00 out of the money that I was responsible for processing and depositing. Well, had I not caught it, Well, you knew what she was going to do. She was going to blame me. Well, guess what? I had a meeting with the principal, supervisor, and the employee. I stated and proved that the Caucasian employee had stolen the $40.00 and had I not discovered it, she was going to blame me because I was responsible for the money. This witch tried to sabotage me and get me fired. Even though, the employee admitted to taking the money in the meeting, the principal did not say anything to her or terminate her. I thought this was the most ridiculous thing. Talk about corruption, this was it!

The person in charge did absolutely nothing.

People need to look at these people who supposed to be in charge. If some of these people are removed, things might go better.

We should always look to do better and not just settle for a position because it comes along. Again, problems bring opportunities. Even though, we don't like problems. Problems are a part of Life. I am now more creative, stronger, and wiser. I will always strive for better opportunities.

Speaking of evil people, there is someone who constantly burglarizes and vandalizes my house and damages my cars and my yard. I reported these crimes to the police and nothing was done to this person. The police chief refused to do anything to this criminal. That is the reason why I am dealing with these crimes. Some people are in positions and shouldn't be. Eventually, this criminal will get what is coming to him.

7

ESSENTIAL ELEMENTS

I read a book, *"It Only Takes a Minute to Change Your Life,"* by Willie Jolley. In this book, it was a question: Time is moving, are you? Well, I immediately thought: No, I am not moving and time has passed me by.

I remember as if it were yesterday when I was pledging AKA at Alabama A&M University. I was Miss AKA, Time has gone by. One thing about time, once it is gone, it is gone; it cannot be replaced. That is why if there is something that I want to do, I am going to try to do it. There is no time for procrastination or excuses. I should try to make things happen. Even if things don't happen the way that I want them to, I should definitely try to put forth effort to what I want. If I don't, then who will? I am not where I want to be and maybe, I will get there soon. I would like to be in a position that I will enjoy and, of course, make a lot of money.

As I kept reading this book, it asked several more questions: What are you doing with your minutes? Do you use them wisely, or do you squander your precious minutes? Do you fill your life with time a-wasting, or do you fill your time with a-making?

I have been time a-wasting. I have been wasting a lot of my minutes. I should have been life a-making. Perhaps, my Life would have been better and I would have been in a better position if I had focused more on my time and used it wisely. It's not how much time you have, but what you do with the time you've got.

I now realize that I need to use my minutes wisely and that each minute counts. From a great minute comes a great hour, and from a great hour comes a great day, and from a great day comes a great week, then a great month, then a great year. From there, I can navigate, achieve my goals and dreams, and have a better life.

No matter where we are in life, we do have a choice. I must use my time wisely and try to make better choices. I must use my time wisely and try to make better choices.

No matter where I am in life, I have to make a choice to change things and go after my goals. I don't need to worry about the bad people that I have encountered in the past, both on these jobs and personally. I need to stop looking in the past and look to the future. I have to look at the bigger picture and know that my best is yet to come.

Willie Jolley was on the Public Broadcasting System Channel. He stated that age has nothing to do with your success. He talked about Colonel Sanders was in his 60s when he opened his first Kentucky Fried Chicken. He stated that Life is going to knock you down and you have to get back up. I am glad that I have a chance to get back up and do it right and go after what I want.

Michelle Obama told Merced graduates that you will have setbacks, you will make mistakes. There is no clear pathway to your vision.

After having setbacks and making mistakes, I am smarter and stronger and now in a position where I can make better and wiser decisions. I am now seeing the vision clearer.

8

THE COOKOUT

I wanted some Barbeque Ribs for the Memorial Day weekend. I thought about going to Sonny's Barbeque to get some ribs because it was nobody but me. That Sunday, day before Memorial Day, I woke up and decided that I would barbeque myself. I felt as though it would be good for me, mentally.

The meteorologists had predicted rain for the Memorial Day weekend for the next eight days. I went to the grocery store. While I was in the grocery store, a man came and stood beside me. We were standing side by side looking at the baby back ribs. I told the man, "You know it look as if it is about to start raining." He told me Yeah, but it will be okay as long as I have made my fire before the rain starts. Well, I thought about what the man said. I thought it will be okay as long as I make my fire before it rains.

Well, I purchased my baby back ribs, bake beans, charcoal, and other items that I needed for my "cookout." I even bought ground beef because I like hamburgers on the grill. I like the smoke taste. My sister had bought me a Portable Tabletop Charcoal Grill and I was going to use it for the first time.

I first marinated my ribs because that was what I was focusing on because I really wanted some Barbeque Ribs. I went on to put the Charcoal Grill together. As I read the instructions, it said not to put the grill on top of wood and any combustible objects. Well, everything was either wood or combustible. I have to get an aluminum stand or steel stand next time when I use my Portable Tabletop Charcoal Grill. I thought that I could put the charcoal grill on top of my long grill that I use to cook pancakes on.

I proceeded to start my fire. I used some cheap charcoal, instead of my Usual, Kingsford Match and Light Charcoal! This was a wrong move.

I had the Portable Tabletop Charcoal Grill on the long grill on my patio deck. As the fire was blazing, it was spreading pretty wildly. I asked God if I get through this, I will not use the grill on the patio deck until I have a steel or aluminum stand for my portable grill. I was okay once the fire stopped blazing and went normal. I then put my Baby back ribs on the grill. It began to rain about 30 minutes later. I waited until it stopped raining and went on the patio deck to check my ribs. I stooped down to look at my ribs on the grill because I didn't have a stand to put my grill on. Guess what? The fire had gone out. It was only burning in one spot.

Well, I had to make a 2nd fire. I decided to move the charcoal grill in front of my house and place the grill on the walkway on the concrete. This would be better.

I had to bend over to start my fire and it took a while to light up. This store brand charcoal was part of the problem. The charcoal finally ignited. I waited about 20 minutes for the fire to go down. As I was waiting, I decided that I was going to put some hamburgers on the grill with the ribs to cook at the same time because I was really, really hungry. I thought that I could rush it and be able to eat something sooner than later. Well, that did not work out. When I put the hamburgers on the grill, the grease from the hamburgers started a fire. When I moved the hamburgers to another spot on the grill, another fire started under them. I had to rush in the house and put some water on the fires. The fires started back up again. I had to finally take my hamburgers off the grill and just cook my ribs, alone.

Well, my Barbeque Ribs finally got done. I took them off the grill. I went back in the house and got my hamburgers to put them on the grill. As I was putting my hamburgers on the grill, it appeared that the charcoal wasn't burning. But, I waited to see what would happen. It started to rain again. I went out in the rain. I had a plastic bag on top of my head. I was stooping down to look at my hamburgers. I was right; the fire had gone out, again.

By this time, a lady visiting the next door neighbor came out and said, "You are barbequing in the rain." At this time, I was beginning to feel disgusted. I removed the raw hamburgers off the grill.

I begin to talk to God, again. I said, "God, you are trying to tell me something here." Then something popped into my mind, "Yeah, you have to have Persistence and Determination."

Well, I proceeded to use Persistence and Determination and started my 3rd fire. I put my hamburgers on the grill. As my hamburgers were cooking, I proceeded to make me a plate because I was hungry. I had Baby back ribs, bake beans, and coleslaw. I ended up eating the ribs first.

My hamburgers finally got done. It was good timing because it looked like the fire was going out, again. My dinner was really good! I did a good job, and I hung in there and got good results! My food was delicious. Despite the weather and the fire kept going out, I persisted on having a delicious Barbeque.

I Learned Several Things During My BARBEQUE COOKOUT.

1. It might take you a while to reach your goals. I started at 3:00 p.m., and I finished at 7:00 p.m.
2. It does not matter what time or how long it takes to "Reach Your Goals" as long as you reach them.
3. You have to have Persistence and Determination in order to "Reach Your Goals."
4. Even though I had obstacles, I did not stop. I continued to "Reach My Goals."
5. I also learned not to try to save a few dollars and get cheaper charcoal. I should have gotten the good stuff; the kind of charcoal that I normally use.

I now know that I have to have Persistence and Determination in order to "Reach My Goals." I will apply this to my Life.

I must have Persistence, Determination, A Strong Desire, and Action in everything that I do in my life and in "Reaching my Goals and Dreams."

Even though I was tired from bending over and stooping down while grilling, at the end, I had accomplished my goals. I got what I wanted. I enjoyed some good Barbeque Ribs and hamburgers on the grill.

MY MISSION WAS ACCOMPLISHED!

LIVING THROUGH OBSTACLES and overcoming them will allow me to reach my goals.

KEEP PUSHING

My "Cookout" taught me a lot. I know that you should never give up. No matter what, you should never give up. Things might not go exactly as planned, but continue on until you reach your goal. Encouragement is good. It is good to have good friends to encourage you, but it is rare. I have to keep pushing. It is hard sometimes.

I have heard people say, A delay is not a denial. This means that I can accomplish my goals and dreams.

Life is full of obstacles and challenges. You never know what road or pathway life is going to take you. I sure did not know that my life would take this pathway. I figured that I would be successful many years ago. I don't know what God has for me. He had put me with many fools in my lifetime. Well, I don't know if I can say that God did it, but I can say that there are a lot of fools out there. It always seems that I get the fool to work under or with. Another example, I had gotten a job at a large major healthcare institution. I was okay with the first supervisor.

They created a new department and they wanted me to work in it. Problems then began. I was put with a fool. The manager of this new department had just started working there. This person didn't know anybody or anything. This new hired person sent me an email informing me that she wanted me to come to her building to meet her. Well, I really didn't want to do it because I figured it was something up with this. I went to the building where she was. She wanted to know about me. I told her about my education and work experiences. She was jealous of me and my education and work experiences. People on these jobs will try to sabotage you, try to get you fired, and mess you up because they are threatened. You also have people who don't want to see you thrive and succeed. After I told her my qualifications, she did not have anything to say after that. The meeting suddenly came to an end. As I walked out of her office, I wondered what was going to happen next.

Well, I was right! This new manager was jealous of me. Note, I had only met and seen her for the first time when she told me to come to her office so that she could meet me. The next week, three days after meeting her, the new manager called me to tell me to walk across the street to come to her office again. I was wondering why she was calling me to come to her office. Note, I never saw the woman but that one time. I walked in the other building to her office; this woman had a write-up ready for me. This person didn't know me from a can of paint. I could not believe this. This woman did not know anything about me, but my qualifications: what I had told her about me. I did not know anything about her. But, I was quickly finding out how she was. She was foolish. She had written me up, stating that I talk too loud on the telephone. And she was located in a different building and she just got hired. Note, this new manager never saw me at work and she did not know how I performed on my job. Plus, she was in a different building. This was a way that she could say something negative about me. Well, I did not sign the write-up and I put my comments on the little write-up. I wrote that it was three of us in a very small room and that I hear the other two employees talking when I talk on the phone. Naturally, if we sit under each other, voices are going to carry. Well, the write-up did not go anywhere because of the comments that I wrote on it. This new person continued her nonsense simply because she had problems within herself i.e. jealousy, inferiority, racism, and mental problems.

The point was: The new manager was jealous of me. I had more education and experience than she did and she was the manager. That happens a lot. She was not educated. She did not have any experience in healthcare business. In fact, she never worked at a healthcare institution in her life. The bottom line, this new manager knew that I was much smarter, more educated, and much knowledgeable than she was. She felt inferior to me. She was white and so were the director and assistant.

This person told the employees to use to the back door only and not to use the front door of the building and to use the copy machine in the back of the building only and not to walk to the front of the building at all.

One day, another employee and I walked to the front of the building to make copies because the copy machine in the back wasn't working. This new manager, sitting at her desk in her office, shouted, "Is the other copy machine not working?" I did not say anything. The other employee, stated, "Well, that is what they say," instead of her saying, "No." This other employee never stood up. As a matter of fact, I believe this employee was the one who lied on me at the very beginning about me talking too loud on the telephone when it was only three of us in a very, very small office- the size for one person. Everybody's voice carried throughout the tiny office; we were sitting on top of one another. This employee wanted me in trouble for some reason. She had a problem, too.

Well, the next day, I walked to the front of the building to use the copy machine because the copy machine in the back was still not working. As I was getting ready to use the copy machine in the front of the building, Diana, the new manager, shouted out of her office, "Is the copy machine in the back working." I said, "No, it is not." Diana proceeded to come out of her office and she wanted me to walk back to the copy machine in the back. She walked with me as to say that I did not know what I was talking about. Well, we got to the back copy machine and Diana asked the other employee was the copy machine working, and that employee told her, "No.' as we were standing up there, Diana proceeded to try to make copies anyway after I and the other employee told her that it did not work. This was how foolish she was. After Diana tried to make copies on the broken copy machine, I looked at her and she felt foolish and she was. That was the problem, Diana and the other management individuals knew that they weren't smart and that I knew more than they did. They were right. They felt inferior to me.

Diana and her crew weren't up on their history. They didn't know that Abraham Lincoln had freed the slaves. Abraham Lincoln wrote the Emancipation Proclamation. Abraham Lincoln freed all slaves by 1865.

Rosa Parks refused to give up her seat on a Montgomery bus on December I, 1965 which created the Montgomery Bus Boycott led by Martin Luther King, Jr. which led us to be able to sit, stand, and go where we want to.

I have had jealous supervisors who were white and black.

Jealousy and ignorance have no color. I have had other employees who were jealous. They were haters. This happens a lot. I have had to deal with stupid, jealous, envious supervisors, employees, and other people a lot. Let's face it, there are people who don't want to see you get ahead and are jealous and envious of you, and jealous of your knowledge and education. I have run into a lot of those people.

As an educator, I got a chance to touch many students' lives and help them. I had good moments.

As I told you, life has been different for me. I don't know why life took me down this pathway so many times. It seemed like every time, I always get the fool to work with. Some things you just don't understand in life and this is one of them. Life is very unpredictable.

The main thing is to close the door on the past and to look to my future. Let God handle those fools that had done me wrong in the past. I need to look ahead and move forward. I need to seek better things ahead.

10

LIFE IS ABOUT CHOICES

Life is about choices. Well, I made some bad choices. Taking the wrong jobs, making the wrong decisions, thinking that certain people were my friends, dating and marrying the wrong person, and taking wrong advice from the wrong person are some of the bad choices that I made in life. Over thinking, worrying, and fear can mess you up and cause you to make bad choices and decisions. You tend to make the wrong decision if you make the decision while you are upset and emotional. I listened to people that I shouldn't have. I definitely shouldn't have listened to people who I didn't like and they told lies to me. I listened, trying to prevent things from happening and listening to those people who were trying to sabotage me and who didn't have my best interest at heart. I have definitely learned my lesson. Some people are just jealous of you and don't want to see you thrive and move ahead. I got it now. Again, I have learned my lesson. Sometimes, making wrong choices will set you back. I thank God for my Mom! And I thank God for my Life!

You usually worry about people on the street who could do you harm or try to take advantage of you. Your husband, friend, or someone else you know can do you wrong as well. I had jewelry missing, was lied to and other situations happened during this time. He was jealous, malicious and didn't have my best interest at heart. It was too bad that I didn't know how this person was before I spent my time and money. He did not want me to have anything and did not want me to have any happy moments. He never had my best interest at heart. I will never make this mistake again. Sometimes, when you are in relationships, you don't know what you are really into. You really don't know the person. You can be good to a person and then the person would turn around and do you wrong and take advantage of you. I will get it right the next time. Next time, I will do research on an individual, get a private investigator, get credit and history reports. etc. I will be on top of my game. I will do what Judge Mablean says, 'Look Before I Leap." I don't need dead weight. I want more for my Life. I need someone who would treat me like a Queen and to help uplift and to help my life to be better. I would not have wasted any time with this individual. I wasted time and money. I could have been doing other things. My Mom gave us an expensive and illustrious wedding reception. This was a very special day for me. My family members, Mom, Dad, sisters, and brother, aunts, nephews, uncle, and my Godmother Totsie were there with me. The wedding reception was beautiful. I felt like a princess on that day. Later on, I discovered I had a toad frog. I will always remember the beautiful wedding reception that my beautiful mother gave me and I will always remember and love my mother!

11

LIFE IS ABOUT CHOICES, PART II– FYI

I was looking at TV; I saw a case where a young couple from Alabama had gotten married and went on their honeymoon in Australia. Apparently, the young lady did not know her husband, either. Her new husband killed her. They were only married for eleven days. He told the wife before they went on their honeymoon to change her life policy to the max, $130,000, and to change the beneficiary from her dad to him. The young lady talked it over with her dad and the dad told her not to do it and to wait until she came back from her honeymoon and then change the policy.

Her dad told her to tell her husband that she had already changed the policy. That was a good idea, given that the husband killed her on their honeymoon. The husband was a rescue diver and he told the young lady that if she wanted to be with him, she had to start scuba diving. They went scuba diving together and while they were in the water, the husband detached his wife's oxygen tank. The wife immediately went to the bottom and the husband was right next to her looking at his wife drown and he swam to the top.

Being a rescue diver, he could have brought her up to the

top of the water when he surfaced. To top it off, at the burial site, the husband kept removing flowers that his deceased wife's family put on her grave. The family members were wandering who was removing the flowers off the grave. The deceased young lady's dad put another flower on the grave and bolted down with barb wire. The police had put surveillance camera next to the grave site. The husband was caught walking with barb wire cutters and cutting the barb wire and removing the flowers and throwing them in the trash can. The husband reminded me of someone who was sneaky.

The husband pleaded guilty to manslaughter and he only was sentenced to prison for eleven months in Australia.

There are a lot of women who don't know who they married until later on. Some of the husbands wound up being different people i.e. thieves, murderers, liars, and other things. I can relate to the thieves and liars.

Apparently this is abundant; I saw another show entitled, "The Years of Living Dangerously." This lady had been married to her husband for eleven years. She said that she wanted to know who the man that she was married to was. I will call the lady, Lora. Lora's husband was always putting her in danger. One day, her husband told her to take a sleeping to make her feel better. Although she didn't want to do it, she said that she said, okay and took the sleeping pill. The husband wanted her to go to the store and he told her that he would drive her because she had just taken the sleeping pill. While driving the car, the husband sped up and was driving very fast. Lora told her husband to slow down, but he kept on driving faster. The husband kept on driving faster and had an accident. This did not kill Lora. The husband told her that he was a college professor. Well, that was not true. When Lora had planned on going to the college to see her husband lecture, he told her that he did not feel well. Lora told him to go on and that he would feel better. Instead, the husband took some pills and pretended like he was having a heart attack. He asked Lora to help him down the stairs and both of them fell to the bottom. Her husband told her that he was an Admiral in the Navy. He also told her that he was a missionary.

The husband talked Lora in going on an Egyptian trip. While her husband was taking a shower in the hotel, Lora saw a bottle of liquid with no label and some plastic gloves on the counter. She asked her husband what was the liquid and he told her ether. She asked him what he was going to do with it. He told her that he was going to rub it on his neck because the doctor told him to. Lora said that she knew that ether was deadly. She thought that was strange to put ether on his neck. Later on, the husband pinned her down and tried to kill her by pouring ether on her. Lora barely got away by running to the desk for help and telling the person to call the police and tell them that her husband tried to kill her. Lora later discovered that her husband was not an Admiral in the Navy nor a college professor, nor missionary. She found out that her husband was the black sheep of the family. Her husband got kicked out of the military and he never did pass boot camp. He never got out of training. Her husband only served a short stint in jail and a year probation. When her husband got out of jail, Lora was scared and she thought that the husband would come after her even though she had a protection order. Her husband married again. Lora sent a message to his new wife and told her to be careful and that he was going to try to kill her, too. The husband ended up killing himself by accident. He was trying to take some pills and pretend like he was having another heart attack to fool his new wife, and mixed the wrong concoction of pills together and took an overdose. Lora now has a new husband and speaks to women groups.

In Life, you learn that everybody does not have your best interest at heart. Some people do not want you to succeed; they want you to fail. For I know this all too well. I have had many years of bad bosses and supervisors who have harassed me, tried to sabotage me and tried to get me fired for no reason. They were crazy, jealous and malicious. I have had to deal with jealous and malicious employees, too; they would tell lies on me to try to get me in trouble. If it didn't happen to me, I wouldn't believe what people would actually do.

I AM NOW IN A BETTER PLACE.

I read in a book that problems only create better opportunities. I have gotten the opportunity to use my talents and skills to write this book; this is a wonderful opportunity. I would like to be a TV Host or Analyst. I can do it! I welcome new opportunities. The right people need to contact me and give me an opportunity. My dreams can be fulfilled.

Life has taken me down a different pathway and the pathway of the unknown and the pathway of problem people, I will not let people or circumstances bring me down or stop my success.

I will soar like an eagle! I am on my way! Success is mine.

LIFE IS ABOUT CHOICES, PART III

"Life is like a box of chocolates; you never know what you are going to get."

This is indeed one of my favorite quotes. This is so true. I think about this quote all the time. This is so fitting. In life, you don't know what you are going to get sometimes.

Life is about choices. Sometimes, you are not going to know if your choice or choices are going to be good or bad until after you have made your choice or choices. I majored in marketing in college. Now, I would have done something different if I could change things. At that time, I wanted to major in business. If I could change the hands of time, I would have majored in another area. I believe that I would have been good as a lawyer. I am analytical and pay close attention to details. I believe in justice and being fair. As you live life, you later on discover things that really interest you and the good qualities that you have inside of you.

There are opportunities that I would like to try: TV Host, Analyst, acting.

Honesty, Loyalty, Good character, Good mannerisms, and Integrity are attributes that I'm seeking in a friend or mate.

In a friendship or relationship, "I have to look before I leap." I now think about Judge Mablean's quote.

LIFE'S LESSON

Life is your best lesson. I have learned a lot in my Life. I will pay attention to some things. You might want to take heed.

1. If I am interested in someone, I am going to make sure that I meet his parents. The fruit does not fall too far from the tree.
2. I will pay attention to how a person treats me.
3. I will analyze whether this person cares about my feelings and well-being. Does this person pay attention to my needs and surprises me with gifts or takes me out and do some things that I like to do.
4. I will analyze whether this person makes me a better person, is this person positive and has good values and good character,
5. I will assess whether this person has good energy and brightens my day and mood.

13

MAKING DECISIONS

Decision-making is a part of life. Sometimes, we all make bad decisions. I can truly say that I have made some bad decisions. Fear and anxiety can cause you to make bad decisions. Overthinking can cause you to make bad decisions. Not thinking things through, not thinking about the pros and cons can lead to bad decisions. Taking bad advice and listening to the wrong individuals who want to see you fail can cause you to make bad decisions. I have taken wrong advice from the wrong individuals and it set me back a long time. I have learned my lesson. I will focus on what I need to do. I got it now! I won't waste my time with losers! As I reflect on bad decisions, I thought if I would have made better decisions and choices, my life would have been better. Oh, well. I have to think things thoroughly. I am moving forward!

I wish that I had known and utilized the 5-step decision-making process, which includes the following steps: Ask clarifying questions, Gather information, Evaluate options, Make a final decision, and Review the results. I took a teaching position without executing the 5 step decision-making process.

I was at a new school and I was given a mentor. Well, she

really wasn't a mentor because this person tried to sabotage me instead of trying to help me like she supposed to have done. The principal had us to complete some forms. As I was completing my forms at my desk, this mentor entered my classroom and interrupted me to tell me to complete the forms incorrectly intentionally and then she told me after I'm done to turn them in to her when in fact, I suppose to turn the forms into the principal not her. I completed the forms correctly and turned the forms into the principal like I was supposed to do and I also gave the so-called mentor a copy like she said. She looked funny when she saw that I completed the assignment correctly and I didn't listen to her wrong instructions. She should have felt stupid. This so-called mentor was planning on going to tell the principal that I didn't know what I was doing. Well, I fixed her. She saw that I did know what I was doing. There are people who don't want you to succeed and they want to see you fail like this individual. There are low-down people in this world.

When I arrived in Selma and saw the notorious Pettus Bridge, as I was about to drive over the bridge, I immediately thought about "Bloody Sunday." Flashes appeared before my eyes. In my vision I saw the police attack Martin Luther King, Jr., Congressman John Lewis, and other marchers with dogs and water hoses. The marchers were falling down and beaten with batons and sticks and being trampled on. This was something else. I actually saw the vision; it was like I was there on "Bloody Sunday." It was a unique bad feeling. That was probably my cue that I wasn't supposed to have been there. I was offered another job which I should have taken. That was my first time being in Selma, Alabama. Everybody knows about the Pettus Bridge and "Bloody Sunday." That made history all over the world. It is still part of History.

As I drove across the Pettus Bridge, I asked myself, "What have I done?" I realized that I had made another bad decision.

Luckily, I did not have to drive over the Pettus Bridge every day. When I got to my classroom, I asked myself again, "What have I done?" Decisions, Decisions, Decisions, we all make some bad ones. If we had a crystal ball or had a map to Life, we would know which way to go and which way or people to avoid. I guess God did not design it to be easy. I believe it would have been helpful for me. I guess that you would not have any surprises or upsets. I like the good surprises, but I could live without the upsets. But this goes with Life, too.

I was hired to teach Language Arts, seventh grade. Well, after I had made the move to Alabama, an hour away from Selma, after I had signed an apartment lease, after I had paid the movers to move me, and after I attended a week of orientation, the principal then told me that I would be teaching Accelerated Core and not Language Arts, and that I would be teaching eighth grade. This was the wrong time to be telling me this news. I should have been notified of these changes prior to my moving and accepting this job. At that point, I had no choice but to stay and work in that teaching position.

Accelerated Core was something new. This course was supposed to be a computer class designed to teach students the skills needed for the high school graduation exit exam.

Well, I had to improvise the whole time that I was at this school. This was new to me, being in a teaching position with no textbooks, computer, resources, or anything else. Furthermore, there were no computers for the classes, and I didn't have a computer either. I later got a computer weeks later. I really had to be creative. I did well! I had strong classes without any textbooks and resources. I did a good job if I must say so myself. My classes were successful despite the lack of resources from the school. Teaching these classes brought out my creativity. I taught this class without any books or materials. I had to bring in my own resources. Teaching these classes with no materials and being in this position have taught me that I am creative and that I can be in control in bad situations, that I can be successful, and do anything.

I thought that God sent me there, but I was wrong. That wasn't God; that was me. It was a mistake.

Perhaps I am stronger, but I don't want to be in this position again.

I have learned a lot of things in my lifetime. One thing in life that is for sure is that you can't trust everybody and that some people are envious.

The mentor told me to fill the paperwork out wrong intentionally, but I filled it out the correct way. I was wondering why this person would tell me the wrong way. This mentor wanted me to look bad. Again, I filled the paperwork out correctly. I knew what I was doing!

The mentor never tried that on me again. In fact, she kept her distance. She knew that I knew what she was trying to do.

There are a lot of people who try to mess you up and try to sabotage you. I have encountered a lot of these people which have included managers, principals, supervisors, and colleagues. Be Aware! For I know this all too well. Some people try to make you look like you are doing something wrong and it is them all along who is doing wrong.

My mentor told me that she was a preacher. I knew right then and there that many are called and few are chosen. If she was a preacher, why did she tell me to do the wrong thing so that I could look bad? She wasn't doing the right thing. What type of preacher is this, and what type of mentor is this?

While I was teaching my class, my so-called mentor came in

and interrupted my class to put desks in four students groups whereby having eighth grade students facing each other like elementary students. I asked her what she was doing. She stated that the principal wanted everybody to put their desks in groups facing each other. This was inappropriate for her to come barging in my class and interrupting my class to move desks around and furthermore, this was not her classroom; it was mine. That was up to me to move the desks.

This mentor was no mentor. She was no help; she was everything but. It was a good thing that I knew what I was doing.

One particular morning, I told the Assistant Principal that I was going to have a good day. I guess he went and told the Principal that I said that I was going to have a good day. Well, I looked up, and there the Principal was. She had started to harass me. She usually started early in the morning, messing with me.

The school system had a pretty good superintendent at that time. The superintendent handled her business; she got rid of this problem. She nipped it in the bud. We need more leaders like this.

The Principal never harassed me anymore. I could go to work every day without being harassed by the Principal.

14

A BETTER LIFE!

Many people are facing hardships and obstacles in today's society. Many people are struggling with the economy, losing their jobs or have lost their jobs, struggling to find a job, struggling with foreclosure on their homes, struggling with homelessness, struggling without healthcare, struggling to pay their bills, struggling to make ends meet, or just plain struggling.

We all face something. Obstacles are inevitable. Some people have it harder than others.

Through my storms, I had many blessings or still have many blessings. I have been blessed to have had a loving, wonderful, and supporting mother to provide me with necessities to survive, and to have come from a good family. I am blessed to have my health and strength. I am fortunate to have a Bachelor's Degree and to be able to have gone to college to get a higher education. With life experiences, I feel that I am a wiser and stronger person.

I thought that things would have been better and easier for me. Life doesn't come with a road map or with any instructions. You never know what pathway that you are going to take in Life. It can be good or bad.

They say that whatever you go through, it is designed to make you stronger and after the rain, there is a rainbow or sunshine.

Sometimes, I believe that timing is a factor and some things are not going to happen until it is time. Sometimes, you can try hard as you might and things won't budge. But, you should definitely try.

THE TIME IS NOW!
IT IS TIME FOR ME TO BE
SUCCESSFUL AND PROSPEROUS!
AND TRY OTHER THINGS